AF226557

Body Language in Car Sales

How Posture, Eye Contact, and Presence Build Customer Trust

Bruce Huddleston

Bedrock Heritage Publishing

ISBN: 978-1-972179-12-3

EPUB: 978-1-972179-61-1

Published by Bedrock Heritage Publishing

A Division of Life Guidance Consulting LLC

Tyler, Texas

www.bedrockheritagepublishing.com

info@bedrockheritagepublishing.com

Manufactured in the United States of America

DISCLAIMER

This book is based on the author's personal and professional experiences, observations, and opinions accumulated over a thirty-five-year career in the automotive industry. It is intended for educational and informational purposes only.

The stories and anecdotes contained in this book are drawn from real-world situations encountered throughout the author's career. However, names, identifying details, specific circumstances, employer names, dealership names, and individual characteristics have been changed, omitted, combined, or fictionalized to protect the privacy of the individuals involved. Any resemblance to specific living persons, current or former employers, or existing businesses is coincidental and unintentional.

No individual, dealership, organization, or employer referenced or implied in the stories within this book has reviewed, approved, or endorsed the content herein. The recollections and characterizations presented are solely the author's own perspective and memory of events and do not constitute a factual record, legal testimony, or statement of fact regarding any identifiable person or entity.

The sales strategies, techniques, and professional advice presented in this book reflect the author's personal approach and experience. Individual results will vary based on experience, effort, market conditions, dealership policies, and other factors beyond the author's control. Nothing in this book constitutes a guarantee of income, employment, or professional outcome.

The author and publisher have made reasonable efforts to ensure the accuracy of information presented at the time of writing. The author and publisher make no representations or warranties regarding the completeness, accuracy, or current applicability of the information contained herein, and expressly disclaim any liability arising from the use or application of the content of this book.

By reading this book, you acknowledge and agree that the author and publisher shall not be liable for any damages, losses, or claims arising directly or indirectly from the use of or reliance upon any information contained herein.

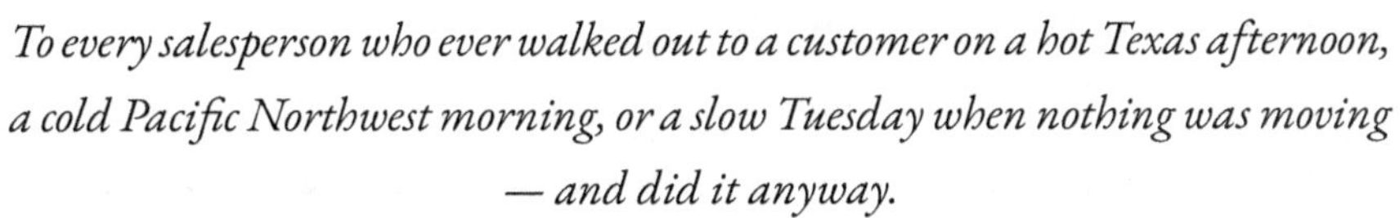

To every salesperson who ever walked out to a customer on a hot Texas afternoon, a cold Pacific Northwest morning, or a slow Tuesday when nothing was moving — and did it anyway.

The floor is unforgiving. You already know that. What most people never figure out is that the customers are reading you before you say a word. This book is for those who want to understand what they're saying.

Free Bonus For Readers

Your Complete Digital Script Library

Get the Car Sales Survival Quick-Reference Card — a free companion to this book that puts the key rules and techniques on one page you can keep at your desk.

www.carsalessurvivalseries.com/scripts
Enter your email to claim your free reader bonus.
Print it. Keep it. Use it.

CONTENTS

Introduction

What Your Body Says Before You Open Your Mouth

Most salespeople think selling starts when they open their mouths. It doesn't.

It starts the moment the customer sees you.

Before you say hello, before you introduce yourself, before you ask a single question — the customer has already formed an impression. They've clocked your posture. Your pace. The look on your face. Whether you seem relaxed or like you're about to tackle them. All of that registers in the first few seconds, and it happens automatically. They're not doing it consciously. Their brain is doing it for them.

I've been in this business for thirty-five years. I've managed many showrooms, trained hundreds of salespeople, and observed thousands of customer interactions from every angle. And I can tell you this with complete confidence: more deals get hurt in the first thirty seconds than in any negotiation that follows.

Not because of what someone said. Because of what their body said.

The good news is that body language is a skill. It's not a personality type. It's not something you're born with. It's something you can understand, practice, and control. And once you do, the whole front end of a sale gets easier. Customers relax faster. Conversations open up. You stop fighting resistance that was never really about the car.

This book covers the ground. What you're sending before you speak. What customers are sending back. The mistakes that kill deals before they start. And a practical system for using your physical presence as a selling tool.

Read it, then go to work. The floor is the best classroom there is.

"The Rule: The sale begins the moment the customer sees you. Everything your body does from that point forward is part of the presentation."

Chapter 1

Why Body Language Matters More Than Your Words

Here's something that took me a while to appreciate fully, even after years on the floor: when there's a conflict between what someone says and what their body is doing, people believe the body. Every time.

You can say "I'm glad you're here" with a flat expression and slumped shoulders, and the customer hears the opposite. You can say "take all the time you need" while hovering three feet away and shifting your weight from foot to foot, and they feel the pressure before you've said another word.

Research on this has been ongoing for decades. Mehrabian's numbers get quoted a lot — the idea that 55 percent of communication is body language, 38 percent is tone, and only 7 percent is actual words. The exact percentages are debated, but the underlying truth isn't: in a face-to-face interaction, especially one where trust is at stake, how you look and sound carries more weight than what you say.

In car sales, trust is always at stake. Customers walk in with their guard already up. They've been sold before. They've dealt with pressure before. Their radar is on from the second they pull into the lot.

What that radar is scanning for isn't your product knowledge. It's whether you feel safe. Whether you're going to respect their time and their budget. Whether they're going to be okay talking to you.

Your body answers those questions before your mouth gets the chance.

That's why body language matters more than your words. Not because words don't matter — they do. But words come later. Body language is the opening statement. And if the opening statement puts them on edge, you're playing catch-up for the rest of the conversation.

I've watched new salespeople deliver a textbook greeting — the right words, the right sequence — and still lose the customer in the first 30 seconds. The words were fine. The body gave them away. Tight shoulders. Rushed pace. Eyes that kept sliding toward the next car coming in.

The customer felt it. They don't need to be able to name it. They just know something is off, and they pull back.

Flip that around. A salesperson who walks out relaxed, at a natural pace, with a genuine expression and steady eyes — that person communicates competence and calm before they've said a word. The customer's guard comes down a notch. They're more open to the conversation. Everything that follows gets easier.

Words are your tools. Body language is the foundation. Build the foundation first.

"The Rule: When what your body says contradicts what your mouth says, the customer believes your body. Make sure they're saying the same thing."

Chapter 2

The First Thing Customers See

BEFORE YOU GET WITHIN twenty feet of a customer, they've already started forming a picture. Not of you specifically — they don't know you yet. Of what they're walking into. Whether this place is going to be the kind of experience they've dreaded or something different.

You are the first data point.

What do they see first? Not your smile. Not your name badge. They see your posture. The way you carry yourself across a parking lot says a lot. Upright, relaxed, moving with purpose — that reads as confidence. Head down, shoulders in, shuffling out as you'd rather be somewhere else — that reads as misery. Customers pick up on both.

They also see your pace. Are you sprinting at them like they're the last customer on earth? That creates pressure. Are you dragging yourself out like it's a chore? That communicates apathy. The right pace is a natural walk — purposeful but unhurried. You're not chasing them, and you're not avoiding them. You're simply coming over to help.

They see your expression. I've seen salespeople walk out with the look of someone walking to a dentist appointment. Not exactly welcoming. A relaxed, genuine expression — not a forced grin, not a poker face — communicates that you're approachable and that this interaction isn't going to be painful.

They see your appearance. I'll be direct about this: how you look matters. Pressed, clean, professional — that signals you take the job seriously. Wrinkled, sloppy, halfway put-together — that signals the opposite. Customers connect appearance to competence. It's not fair, but it's real, and it's happening before you open your mouth.

I worked with a guy once who understood all of this instinctively. He never had expensive clothes, but everything he wore was clean and sharp. On the Pacific Northwest lot where we worked, when the weather turned, he'd come out in a professional raincoat that matched his attire, umbrellas ready, looking completely at ease. While other salespeople were hunching against the rain and grimacing, he looked like he'd planned the whole thing.

Customers noticed. It made them feel like they were in capable hands before he'd said anything beyond hello.

The first thing customers see sets the frame for everything that follows. Make it count.

FROM THE FLOOR

I was sitting in the front lobby of a dealership I managed — with a glass-front wall and a full view of the lot. A car pulled in. Two salespeople inside saw it at the same time. They both jumped up, ran for the door, and literally shoved each other trying to get through it first, pushing and shoving like it was a race.

The customers, still in their car, watched every second of this.

The one who won was out of breath when he got there. He stuck his hand out and started talking before he'd even caught his breath, never looked at the wife, never acknowledged the kids in the back seat. Just started in.

The family looked around for a few minutes and left.

When I asked what happened, the salesperson said: "They were just looking."

No. They were watching. And what they watched told them everything they needed to know about what the next hour would feel like. The sprint didn't just cost a deal; it cost a deal. It answered every one of the customer's silent questions about this place — and none of the answers were good.

"The Rule: The customer sees you before you see them. What they see in those first moments determines whether the conversation is starting uphill or downhill."

Posture: What Standing Like You Mean It Does for a Sale

Posture is the single loudest nonverbal signal you send. Louder than your expression, louder than your pace, louder than what you're wearing. It broadcasts your internal state to anyone watching.

Stand up straight. I know that sounds like something your mother told you. It's also correct. Upright posture with relaxed shoulders signals confidence and ease. It says: I belong here, I'm comfortable, I've done this before. That is exactly what you want a customer to believe on first contact.

The Slouch is the enemy. I've seen it a thousand times — a salesperson approaching a customer with rounded shoulders, head slightly down, like they're bracing for rejection before it's even happened. Maybe they're tired. Maybe they've had three walk-offs in a row. Maybe they just don't realize they're doing it. It doesn't matter. The customer doesn't know any of that. They just see someone who doesn't look confident, and they mirror that energy back.

There's another version of bad posture that's less obvious: the Rigid. Some salespeople, especially new ones, overcorrect. They stand so stiff and straight it looks like they're bracing for an inspection. That's not confidence either. That's tension. Customers feel the difference.

What you're after is relaxed authority. Shoulders back and down — not up by your ears. Weight is balanced evenly. Head level. The kind of posture that says you're comfortable in your own skin and in your environment. That's the posture of someone customers want to deal with.

Posture matters throughout the conversation, not just on the approach. What are you doing when you're standing next to a vehicle with a customer? Are you leaning against it like you're half asleep? Crossing your arms? Standing slightly behind them, which signals deference and uncertainty? Or are you engaged, upright, physically present in the conversation?

Standing like you mean it doesn't require acting. It requires awareness. Most people default to whatever posture feels comfortable, and comfortable is usually whatever they've done their whole lives. If that's the Slouch, it takes conscious effort to change. But it's worth the effort, because posture is operating on the customer every second you're in their line of sight.

Check yourself before you walk out the door. Shoulders down. Head up. Walk like you're going somewhere worth going. That's it. That small shift changes how the customer reads you from the moment they meet you.

"The Rule: Your posture is broadcasting your confidence level to every customer who can see you. Make sure what they're receiving is what you intend to send."

CHAPTER 4

Eye Contact: The Line Between Confident and Creepy

EYE CONTACT IS WHERE many salespeople go wrong, in one of two directions. Either they avoid it — eyes sliding to the car, the lot, anywhere but the customer's face — or they overdo it, holding a stare so fixed and intense that the customer starts looking for an exit.

Both are problems. Let's talk about why.

Avoiding eye contact signals one of two things: discomfort or disinterest. Either you're nervous, which erodes the customer's confidence in you, or you're not really paying attention to them, which is even worse. Customers notice when they're not being looked at. They feel dismissed. They start to wonder if they're being taken seriously.

The overdo is what I call the Death Stare. Unbroken eye contact, no natural glancing away, laser-focused like you're trying to read their thoughts. That's not confident. That's predatory. Customers feel hunted. The guard goes up fast.

What you're after is natural eye contact. What does that look like? You hold eye contact while you're speaking to them and while they're speaking to you. You let your eyes move naturally — to the vehicle, to something they point out, back to their face. You're not staring them down, and you're not avoiding them. You're just present. Engaged. Paying attention.

Here's the thing about eye contact in the greeting, specifically: it needs to happen early. When you're approaching a customer, make eye contact from a reasonable distance — not across the lot, but maybe 20 feet away — and hold it naturally as you walk toward them, that communicates confidence. It says: I see you, I'm coming over, I'm not surprised you're here, and I'm not nervous about approaching you.

Compare that to the salesperson who walks out with their eyes down, looks up only when they're already standing in front of the customer, and then jumps into the greeting. That feels abrupt. There was no lead-in. No acknowledgment from a distance. Just a sudden appearance and a pitch.

Eye contact during the conversation is about listening as much as talking. When a customer is telling you what they're looking for, look at them. Not at your notepad, not at the inventory on your phone. At them. That kind of attention communicates respect. It tells them that what they're saying matters to you. And when customers feel heard, they open up.

The rule of thumb is simple: look at people when you're talking to them and when they're talking to you. Let your eyes move naturally when you're both looking at something together. That's it. That's the line between confident and creepy.

FROM THE FLOOR

The summer heat in Texas is no joke. I was managing a used car lot — no air conditioning on the lot, obviously — and it was one of those July afternoons where the asphalt is soft, and the air feels like a wet towel. A couple pulled in. I watched my newest salesperson sprint out to meet them — which was already the wrong move — and by the time he got to them, he was visibly sweating through his shirt. The customers looked at him, looked at each other, and said they were just looking. He came back inside looking defeated.

I went out. Introduced myself. Said: "Sorry about the heat — let me know if you want to step inside and cool off while we talk." That's all it took. They came inside. We sold them a car in ninety minutes. The first salesperson did everything wrong before he said a word. I did one thing right: I acknowledged where they were before I asked anything of them.

"The Rule: Look at people when you're talking to them and when they're talking to you. Natural eye contact builds trust. Avoiding it kills credibility. Overdoing it kills comfort."

CHAPTER 5

THE HANDSHAKE AND THE FIRST TOUCH

THE HANDSHAKE IS THE first physical contact you have with a customer. It happens fast, and it registers immediately. And yet it's something a surprising number of salespeople either overthink or don't think about at all.

Let's get the basics right. A handshake should be firm but not crushing. Full palm contact, not fingers-only. One or two pumps. That's it. What you're communicating is: I see you, I'm glad you're here, and I'm a professional. That's all the handshake needs to do.

The weak handshake is a problem. The limp, fingers-only, barely-there version reads as either disinterest or low confidence. Customers notice. It creates a vague unease that they probably can't articulate but absolutely feel. It's a small thing that leaves a mark.

The crusher is also a problem, and it's more common with salespeople who've been told to project confidence. Grinding someone's hand isn't confidence. It's aggression. Customers — especially women, and often the customer you just crushed is the decision-maker — will recoil from it. Not outwardly. But internally, the guard goes up.

There's a timing element too. Don't rush the handshake. If a customer has their hands full, or they're getting out of the car, or they're in the middle of a sentence — wait. Thrusting a hand at someone who isn't ready for it creates an awkward scramble. Let the moment develop naturally.

One more thing about first touch: read the room. Some customers — particularly in a post-pandemic world — don't want to shake hands. If a customer doesn't extend their hand, don't force it. A nod and a warm verbal greeting accomplish the same thing. The goal isn't the handshake itself. The goal is the connection it's supposed to create. If you can get there another way, get there.

After the handshake, there's one rule: give space. First physical contact is not an invitation to move closer. Take a half step back. Let the greeting breathe. Crowding someone right after the handshake is one of the fastest ways to create discomfort.

The handshake is a small window. Use it well.

"The Rule: The handshake is the first physical statement you make. Firm, full, brief. Then step back and give them room."

Chapter 6

Pace and Movement: How You Walk the Lot

How you move on the lot is a continuous broadcast. It's not just the approach to the customer—it's everything about how you walk when you're crossing the lot alone, how you move when you're walking beside a customer to a vehicle, how you position yourself when you stop. All of it is being read.

Pace is the most obvious piece. I covered this in Chapter 2 in the context of the first thing customers see, but it goes beyond the initial approach. Throughout the entire interaction, your pace communicates your internal state.

Moving too fast signals anxiety. It says you're chasing something — a commission, a number, a quota. Customers feel the urgency, and they mirror it back as resistance. Moving too slow signals disengagement. It says you'd rather be somewhere else. Neither serves you.

The right pace is deliberate and unhurried. You're moving with purpose, not scrambling. When you're walking with a customer to look at a vehicle, match their pace. Not your pace. Theirs. If they're strolling, you stroll. If they're moving with intent, you move with intent. Walking ahead of them puts you in a position of leading and pulling. Walking beside them puts you in a conversation. That's where you want to be.

There's a common habit I've seen in salespeople who are new or nervous: the drift. They approach, exchange greetings, and then unconsciously start moving. Shifting weight. Taking half steps, inching closer. The customer doesn't see one big invasion of space. They see a slow accumulation of it, and they step back. And then the salesperson inches forward again. And the customer steps back again. It's a slow-motion chase, and it makes people miserable.

The fix is awareness. Plant your feet when you're talking. Don't drift. If you need to move — to show them something on the vehicle, to open a door, to walk around to the other side — move with intention. Get there, stop, and engage. Don't fidget your way around a car.

One thing the best salespeople do well is use movement to break the tension. If a conversation stalls or a customer seems to be closing off, suggesting they walk with you to look at something specific gives everyone a reset. Movement changes the dynamic. Side-by-side is more comfortable than face-to-face for many people, especially those who are guarded. Walking together to look at a vehicle feels collaborative. That's a useful tool.

Walk as you belong on that lot because you do.

"The Rule: Your pace tells customers whether you're chasing them or guiding them. Slow down. Walk with them. Let the lot feel like a conversation, not a foot race."

CHAPTER 7

FACIAL EXPRESSION: WHAT YOUR FACE IS DOING WHEN YOU THINK NOBODY'S LOOKING

HERE'S THE UNCOMFORTABLE TRUTH about facial expression: you seldom know what yours is doing.

Most people have a resting expression they're completely unaware of. For some, it's neutral and approachable. For others, it's something that reads as irritated, bored, skeptical, or exhausted — none of which they feel, but all of which are visible to everyone around them. Customers included.

I've had conversations with salespeople who were genuinely enthusiastic about helping a customer, but whose faces looked like they were doing math they didn't want to do. They had no idea. And the customers they approached had a correspondingly harder time opening up, without knowing why.

The first thing to do is find out what your resting face looks like to other people. Ask a colleague you trust. Better yet, watch yourself on video — most phones can do this now. It's uncomfortable the first time. It's also useful information you can't get any other way.

A genuine smile is your most powerful opening expression. Not a performance smile — customers can spot the difference. The forced retail grin that says, "I have to be here" creates no warmth. A real smile — even a small one — that says I'm actually glad to see you creates immediate openness.

The challenge is generating a genuine smile on a slow Tuesday when you're on your fifth hour of nothing happening. I get it. Here's what I know: the smile doesn't have to come from excitement about the next customer. It can come from intention. You decide to bring that energy because you understand what it does for the interaction. That's not fake. That's professional.

Beyond the opening smile, watch your expression throughout the conversation. What does your face do when a customer says their budget is lower than you expected? When they're on their fourth question about a feature you've explained twice? When they say they want to think about it?

If any trace of frustration, disappointment, or boredom crosses your face in those moments, the customer sees it. And whatever ground you'd built up starts to erode. They feel like a problem instead of a person.

Keep the expression open and engaged throughout. Not fake enthusiasm. Just consistent presence. Eyes that are actually paying attention. A face that communicates: I'm still here, I'm still with you, this is still a good conversation.

Your face is talking every second you're in front of a customer. Make sure it's saying something useful.

FROM THE FLOOR

I walked into a well-known furniture store one afternoon looking for a recliner. Had a specific one in mind. Knew what I wanted to spend. Ready to buy.

Three salespeople were sitting on a showroom couch. I could hear them — in earshot, not trying to be quiet — debating whose turn it was to help me. Like I was an interruption to whatever they had going on.

The one who drew the short straw walked over. No greeting. No name. No smile. Just: "What are you here to buy today?"

I said: "Nothing. I'm just looking. I'll let you know if I need help."

And I meant it. They'd lost me in the first five seconds. I didn't buy a thing there. Went somewhere else and bought the same recliner the same afternoon.

The irony is, I walked in ready to spend money. All they had to do was make me feel like a person, not a chore. Instead, they spent more energy arguing over whose turn it was than they spent on the customer standing in front of them. That's not a sales problem. That's a culture problem. And it starts—and ends—with how a team treats the greeting.

"The Rule: Your face is part of the presentation. Know what it's doing. A genuine expression opens doors. A checked-out expression closes them — usually before you've said a word."

CHAPTER 8

READING THE CUSTOMER'S BODY LANGUAGE

EVERYTHING WE'VE COVERED SO far has been about what you're sending. Now let's talk about what you're receiving.

Customers are broadcasting constantly. The problem is that most salespeople aren't tuned in. They're thinking about their next line, the next question, the next step in the process. Meanwhile, the customer is telling them exactly how they feel — just not with words.

Reading body language isn't a trick. It's attention. It's the discipline of watching the person in front of you rather than running your own internal script. When you do that, customers tell you a tremendous amount.

Start with the arrival. How did they pull in? Fast and purposeful, like someone who knows what they want? Slow and circling, like someone who's still deciding whether this is the right place? Did they park close and walk straight in, or did they sit in the car for a minute first? All of that is information about where they are mentally before you ever make contact.

Watch what they do when they get out. Do they head directly to a specific vehicle? Do they scan the lot broadly? Do they walk close to the cars and look, or do they hang back? Someone drawn to a specific vehicle is telling you where their interest already lies. Someone scanning broadly is still orienting. Your approach and opening should be different for each.

Once you're in the conversation, read engagement. Open posture — body facing you, arms at their sides or relaxed, leaning slightly in — is good. They're engaged. Closed posture — arms crossed, body angled away, weight shifted back — signals discomfort or defensiveness. Don't ignore it and don't panic about it. Adjust.

Customer eye contact is a green light. When they're making eye contact with you, asking questions, responding to what you say — the conversation is alive. When they start looking past you, scanning the lot, checking a phone — something has shifted. You either lost them or something else is competing for their attention. Either way, you need to recalibrate.

Feet are underrated. People's feet often point in the direction they actually want to go. If you're talking to a couple and one of them has their feet angled toward the exit, they're mentally already leaving. That's not a lost cause — it's a signal that the current approach isn't working for that person. Address it.

Don't read one signal in isolation. Read the cluster. Crossed arms alone might just mean they're cold. Crossed arms plus eyes looking away plus weight shifted back plus short answers — that's a cluster that says something's wrong. Look at the whole picture.

The salesperson who learns to read customers stops guessing and starts responding. That's a different job—a better one.

FROM THE FLOOR

One afternoon, a customer pulled into the lot in a taxi. That caught my attention — most people drive themselves in. This one stepped out and walked directly toward a specific vehicle, as if he already knew exactly what he was looking for.

I didn't rush. I stood up, walked out at a normal pace, and gave him a small wave as I crossed the lot. When I reached him, I introduced myself and told him I'd be glad to help if he had any questions.

He told me he'd just gotten off a flight and came straight from the airport. His vehicle was destroyed in a parking lot fire while he was traveling. He'd seen one of our ads and came directly to us. He knew which vehicle he wanted. He just needed to drive it and confirm it.

We took a short test drive. Came back. He asked how to make out the check.

Start to finish, maybe forty-five minutes. The deal was easy because the approach was right. No pressure, no assumptions, no rushing. Just a professional greeting and a willingness to follow the customer's lead.

Not every customer comes in ready to buy. But every customer deserves that same professional opening. You never know which one is going to be the taxi customer — the one who's already decided and just needs someone not to get in their way.

"The Rule: Stop running your own internal script long enough to actually watch the person in front of you. Customers tell you everything you need to know. Most salespeople just aren't listening with their eyes."

CHAPTER 9

OPEN VS. CLOSED: WHAT CUSTOMER POSTURE TELLS YOU

IN CHAPTER 8, I told you to read the cluster, not the single signal. This chapter is about the most important cluster of all: whether a customer is physically open or physically closed, because that one distinction will tell you more about where the conversation stands than almost anything they say out loud.

An open posture looks like this. Body facing toward you. Arms relaxed at the sides or loose in front. Weight balanced or leaning slightly in. Head up, eyes engaged. This is a customer who is present and at least willing to be in the conversation. It doesn't mean they're buying. It means the door is open. Work with it.

Closed posture looks like this. Arms crossed tightly across the chest. Body angled away, one shoulder turned toward the exit. Weight on the back foot. Eyes that keep moving off you. This is a customer who feels defensive, pressured, or uncertain. Something in the interaction — or something they brought with them before they arrived — has put them in a protective stance.

Here is the mistake most salespeople make with closed posture: they push through it. They talk louder. They add more information. They ask more questions. They interpret the closed posture as an obstacle to overcome with volume or persistence. It is not. It is a signal to back off.

Closed posture is the customer's body saying, "I need space." Give it to them. Physically step back a half step. Lower your energy. Ask one simple, low-pressure question and then stop talking. Let the silence sit. More often than you'd expect, a customer who was closed will begin to open when the pressure drops. They don't always announce it. Their body does.

There's a version of closed posture that isn't about you at all. Some customers walk in carrying something — a bad day, a difficult conversation in the car on the way over, anxiety about spending money, a previous bad experience at a dealership. Their arms are crossed, and their face is tight before you've done a single thing wrong. Reading that correctly matters.

The way you tell the difference is by watching what happens over the first two or three minutes. If the posture starts to loosen as the conversation continues and you're not applying pressure, they brought it with them, and it's thawing. If the posture tightens as the conversation goes on, you're doing something that's driving it. Either way, you now know what you're dealing with, and you can respond accordingly.

Couples add a layer to this. Watch both people, and watch how they interact with each other. If one is open and engaged, and the other is closed and distant, the closed one is the real conversation. Address them. Include them. Don't let yourself get drawn into talking only to the person who seems easier to talk to. The person who seems harder to reach is often the decision-maker.

Open or closed. It's the first question to answer every time you're in front of a customer. Everything else follows from there.

"The Rule: Open posture is an invitation. Closed posture is a signal to back off, not push through. Read it correctly and respond to what's actually happening, not what you wish were happening."

CHAPTER 10

THE SIGNALS THAT SAY THEY'RE READY

THERE'S A MOMENT IN almost every good sales conversation where the customer shifts. The guard comes down. The questions get more specific—the energy changes. A lot of salespeople miss it because they're still in presentation mode, still delivering information, still talking when they should be listening and watching.

Learning to read the signals that say a customer is ready is one of the most valuable things you can develop. Not ready to be closed in the high-pressure sense — ready to move forward. Ready to go deeper. Ready for the next step, whatever that step is.

Here's what those signals look like.

They get specific. A customer who was asking broad questions — what's good on this lot, what do people usually get — starts asking narrow ones. What's the payment on this one? Does this come in gray? How long does delivery take? Specificity is interest. When they start narrowing, follow them into the narrow.

They touch the vehicle. This one is underrated. A customer who was keeping their hands in their pockets or their arms folded now reaches out and touches the car. Runs a hand along the door panel. Grips the steering wheel. Opens the trunk. Physical engagement with the vehicle is a significant signal.

The car is starting to feel real to them. Don't interrupt that moment with a pitch. Let it happen.

They start mentally owning it. Listen for the pronoun shift. It goes from that car to this car. From the seats to my seats. From the payment to what I'd be paying. When a customer starts using possessive language about the vehicle, they're already mentally in it. That is a very good place for them to be.

They slow down. A customer who was moving quickly through the lot, scanning broadly, starts to slow. They linger. They come back to the same vehicle twice. They stand in front of it and just look at it. That pause is worth more than ten minutes of conversation. It means something in them is settling.

They ask about the process. What does it look like from here? How long does paperwork take? When could I have it? These questions are not casual curiosity. They're the customer mentally walking themselves through a purchase they're already considering. Answer them directly and without pressure.

Their body opens. I covered open posture in Chapter 9, but it's worth naming it here specifically in the context of readiness. When a customer who was somewhat closed starts to open up physically — arms uncross, body turns toward you, eye contact increases — that shift is telling you something important. The internal resistance is coming down.

When you see these signals, the move is not to accelerate into a close. The move is to stay calm, stay present, and make the next step easy. The customer is doing the work. Get out of the way and let them.

"The Rule: When the customer is ready, they'll tell you — with their body, their questions, and their language. Your job is to be watching closely enough to hear it."

Chapter 11

Common Body Language Mistakes Salespeople Make

Most body language mistakes aren't malicious. They're habits. Things salespeople have been doing for so long, they don't notice them anymore. But customers notice—every time.

Here are the ones I've seen do the most damage.

The Hover. This is the salesperson who can't stop moving toward the customer. They close the distance constantly—not all at once, but in small, steady increments. The customer steps back. The salesperson follows. By the end of the greeting, they've backed the customer against a fender without either of them fully realizing how it happened. Customers experience this as pressure even when the words are perfectly friendly. Plant your feet. Respect the space between you.

The Fidget. Keys rattling in a pocket. A pen clicked open and closed repeatedly. Hands move from pockets to crossed arms to rubbing the back of the neck. Any repetitive nervous movement bleeds anxiety into the interaction. Customers absorb it. They start to feel uneasy without knowing why—still your hands. If you need something to do with them, hold a notepad or keep them loose at your sides.

The Glance Away. You're mid-conversation with a customer, and another car pulls onto the lot. Your eyes go to it. Maybe just for a second. Maybe more. The customer saw it. They just became a second priority. This is one of the fastest ways to lose a customer's trust. They drove here, they're standing in front of you, and you're watching for the next one. Be where you are.

The Crossed Arms. Some salespeople cross their arms out of habit, especially when they're listening. To them, it's just comfortable. To the customer, it reads as defensive, closed off, or skeptical. It puts a wall in the conversation. Keep your arms open. If you don't know what to do with your hands, let them hang naturally. That's enough.

The Lean Out. This happens when a conversation gets uncomfortable — a customer pushes back on price, says they're not ready, asks a question the salesperson doesn't have an answer to. Instead of staying physically present and engaged, the salesperson leans back, shifts their weight to the rear foot, and creates physical distance. The customer reads this as a retreat. Confidence drains out of the interaction fast. Stay in it. Keep your weight forward, and your posture engaged even when the conversation gets hard.

The Phone. I shouldn't have to say this, but I do. Looking at a phone while a customer is talking — or walking toward one — or anywhere in the interaction — is a full stop insult. It doesn't matter if it's to look up information about the vehicle. Step back, explain what you're doing, and do it quickly. But casual scrolling or checking notifications while a customer exists in your vicinity? That's a deal killer and a professional failure.

The Expression Drop. Everything is professional until the customer says something the salesperson doesn't like — their budget is too low, they want a vehicle that's not on the lot, they say they need to think about it. And the salesperson's face shifts. Just slightly. Disappointment. Frustration. Resignation. Customers catch it instantly, and they don't forget it. Whatever they were considering doing, they pull back from it.

The fix for all of these is the same: awareness. You can't correct a habit you don't know you have. Ask someone you trust to watch you work. Watch yourself on video. Notice what your body does in the moments that feel challenging. That's where the habits live, and that's where the work is.

FROM THE FLOOR

I had a colleague who couldn't get any traction with a woman at the used-car lot. She kept saying she was just looking. He couldn't figure out what was off — he'd done everything right as far as he could tell. He came and got me.

I went out, introduced myself, and asked how I could help her.

She said: "God, thank you. I really want to buy this car. But that other guy looks exactly like my ex-husband, and I cannot stand the sight of him."

Nothing to do with the car. Nothing to do with the approach. She knew exactly what she wanted — she just needed a different person in front of her before she was going to let the conversation happen. We tested the vehicle, worked out fair numbers, and she drove home happy.

Don't take "I'm just looking" personally. Don't take it as a verdict. Take it as information — something needs to be adjusted. Sometimes that's your approach. Sometimes it's giving more space. And occasionally it's a different person entirely. All of those are workable. None of them is the end of the deal.

"The Rule: Bad body language habits are invisible to the person who has them and obvious to every customer who experiences them. Find yours. Fix them. The floor will tell you everything if you're paying attention."

Chapter 12

Using Space: Distance, Positioning, and Presence

Space is a language. Most salespeople have never thought about it that way, but customers feel it immediately when someone gets it wrong.

Proxemics — the study of how people use physical space in communication — tells us that most people have a comfort zone of roughly eighteen inches to four feet for professional interaction with someone they don't know well. Inside that zone is personal space. Violate it too fast, and you trigger a defensive response. Stay too far outside it, and the interaction feels remote and impersonal.

In a car sales context, four feet is about right for the initial greeting. That's close enough to be personal, far enough to feel safe. It gives the customer room to breathe. From there, you let the conversation — and the customer — determine whether you move closer or hold the distance.

Distance changes naturally when you're looking at something together. When you and a customer are both examining a vehicle — opening the hood, looking at the interior, checking the cargo space — you're naturally side by side, and the distance compresses without either of you having to make a decision about it. That's comfortable. It's collaborative. You're both focused on the same object, and proximity doesn't feel like pressure.

Face-to-face at close range is a different thing entirely. That's an evaluative position. It's the position of negotiation and confrontation. Customers feel it, and it raises their guard. Side by side, or at a slight angle, is almost always more comfortable for the early stages of a conversation. Save face-to-face for the desk, when numbers are actually on the table, and the conversation has moved into its formal phase.

Positioning matters when there's more than one customer. If you're working with a couple, don't position yourself so that one of them is always slightly behind you. That person feels excluded, and in car sales, the excluded person is almost always the one who stops the deal. Position yourself so you can see and address both of them naturally, without turning your back on either.

There's a concept I think of as presence without pressure. It means being physically available and engaged without crowding the customer's space or making them feel watched. You're nearby. You're attentive. But you're not hovering. If a customer walks away to look at something on their own, let them. Stay within range but give them the moment. When they look up and find you, be there. Calm. Ready. Not impatient.

The customers who feel most comfortable are those who have never once felt physically cornered. They could have walked away at any point, and they chose not to. That's the goal. Make staying feel like a decision they're making, not a situation they're trapped in.

"The Rule: Space is part of the conversation. Give customers room to breathe, and they'll stay longer. Crowd them, and they'll find a reason to leave."

CHAPTER 13

THE BODY LANGUAGE CHECKLIST

EVERYTHING IN THIS BOOK comes down to awareness and habit. You have to know what good looks like before you can build it into your daily routine. This checklist is a practical tool. Use it before your shift, after a tough interaction, or whenever you feel like something in your approach isn't working, but you can't put your finger on what.

Work through it honestly.

Before You Walk Out the Door

Posture. Stand up straight. Shoulders down and back, not hunched or rigid. Head level. Do a quick check before you step onto the lot. Thirty seconds in front of a mirror is worth an hour of coaching.

Appearance. Are you clean and pressed? Shoes acceptable? Everything in place? Customers make a judgment about your competence based on how you look. Make that judgment easy for them.

Expression. What is your face doing right now? Relax it. If your default expression reads as tense or flat, consciously soften it before you go out. You don't need to perform enthusiasm. Just be open.

Energy. Check your internal state. If you're stressed, distracted, or carrying frustration from the last interaction, deal with it before the next one begins. Take a breath. Reset. The customer walking in right now has nothing to do with whatever just happened.

On the Approach

Pace. Are you walking at a natural, unhurried pace? Not sprinting. Not dragging. Purposeful and calm.

Eye contact. Did you make eye contact from a reasonable distance before you arrived? That acknowledges the customer before the greeting even begins.

Hands. Are they out of your pockets? Loose at your sides or carrying something natural like a notepad? Good.

Expression. Relaxed and genuine. You're glad they're here. Make sure your face knows that.

During the Greeting

Handshake. Firm, full palm, one or two pumps. Then step back and give them space.

Distance. Roughly four feet. Let the customer set the tone from there. Don't inch forward.

Eye contact. Natural and engaged. You're looking at them, not around them.

Body angle. Slightly open, not squared up face-to-face like you're about to arm wrestle. Approachable.

During the Conversation

Feet. Are they planted, or are you drifting toward the customer? Stay put unless you're moving with purpose.

Arms. Open. Not crossed. Not stuffed in pockets.

Fidgeting. Keys, pens, phone. None of it. Still, hands read as confident hands.

Attention. Are your eyes on the customer, or are they scanning the lot? Be where you are.

Expression. Still open. Especially if the conversation gets difficult, no expression drops.

Reading the Customer

Open or closed? Read the posture cluster, not just one signal. Respond accordingly.

Engagement signals. Are they asking specific questions? Touching the vehicle? Using possessive language? Slowing down? These are green lights. Follow them.

Resistance signals. Are they stepping back, crossing their arms, looking away? Back off. Reduce pressure. Give space. Let them come to you.

Both people. If you're working with a couple or a group, are you including everyone? Is there someone you've been neglecting? Fix it now.

The Ongoing Habit

Review one interaction per day. Not to beat yourself up. To get better. What did your body do well? What habit showed up that you need to work on?

Ask for honest feedback from a manager, a colleague, or someone who will tell you the truth. Body language habits are almost invisible to the person who has them.

Watch the salespeople who are consistently successful. Not to copy them. To notice what their body does that yours doesn't yet.

"The Rule: Awareness is the whole game. Know what your body is doing. Know what the customer's body is doing. Respond to reality, not assumptions. That's the checklist in one sentence."

CONCLUSION

Your Body Is Always Selling Something. Make Sure It's Selling the Right Thing

You walked into this book with a job that starts the moment a customer sees you. Not when you speak. Not when you hand them your card. The moment they lay eyes on you.

That's either a problem or an advantage. What it is depends entirely on what you do with it.

The salespeople I've watched succeed over thirty-five years in this business weren't always the best talkers. Some of them weren't even close to the best product experts on the lot. What they had was presence. They made people feel comfortable before a word was exchanged. They communicated confidence, availability, and professionalism through nothing more than how they stood, how they walked, and how they looked at people.

That's not a talent. That's a discipline. And disciplines are built, not born.

Here's what I want you to take off this lot:

Your body is always broadcasting. There is no neutral. Every second you're in a customer's line of sight, you are sending information. Make it deliberate.

Customers are always reading. They don't analyze it. They feel it. And what they feel in the first thirty seconds goes a long way toward determining whether they stay or go, open up or shut down, trust you or tolerate you.

The basics are the whole game. Posture. Eye contact. Pace. Expression. Space. The handshake. None of this is complicated. All of it takes practice.

None of it happens automatically for most people — it has to be built into a habit through repetition and honest self-assessment.

Reading customers is a skill you can develop. It takes attention. It takes discipline to stop running your own script long enough to actually watch the person in front of you. When you do that, customers stop being unpredictable and start being readable. That changes everything.

The mistakes are fixable. The Hover. The Fidget. The Glance Away. The Expression Drop. All of it. Awareness is the first step. Nobody fixes a habit they don't know they have.

Go back to the floor with this, not as a list of rules to remember mid-conversation, but as a foundation to build on. Do the checklist before your shifts. Ask for feedback. Watch your best colleagues. Review your own interactions honestly.

Body language isn't a soft skill. It's the first hard skill of sales. Get it right, and everything that follows gets easier.

— Bruce Huddleston

Tips For The Sales Manager

Most managers I've known coach from the desk. They watch the numbers, and when they're off, they call people in to talk about closing ratios, follow-up calls, and financing options. Those things matter. But by the time the numbers are off, the problem usually started a lot earlier — out on the lot, in the first thirty seconds of an interaction the manager never saw.

Body language is where deals die before they start. If you want to improve your team's performance, start watching how they move.

Get Out of the Desk and Onto the Lot

You cannot coach what you cannot see. Spend time watching your salespeople work—not just the greeting, but the whole front half of the interaction. Watch how they cross the lot. Watch what happens to their posture when a customer says something they don't want to hear. Watch their face when a conversation stalls.

You will see things in five minutes of observation that no amount of post-mortem conversation will ever surface.

Know What Good Looks Like

Before you can coach body language, you need a clear picture of what you're looking for. Confident, unhurried approach. Natural eye contact from a reasonable distance. Relaxed posture. Appropriate space given after the greeting. Genuine expression throughout.

When you see it done right, say so. Specific, immediate positive feedback is the fastest way to lock in a good habit. "You walked out to that customer exactly right — good pace, good posture, you made eye contact before you got there" is more useful than any generic encouragement.

Coach the Habits, Not Just the Results

When a salesperson takes a walk-off and comes back in looking defeated, the first question most managers ask is: "What happened?" The salesperson will tell you what was said. That's not usually where the problem lived.

Ask instead: "What did you do when you walked out? How close were you standing? What was your expression when they said they were just looking?" Get them thinking about their physical presence, not just their words. The words are usually fine. The body gave something away.

Use Video When You Can

If your lot has cameras with decent coverage, use them as a coaching tool. Nothing teaches body language faster than watching yourself. It's uncomfortable. It's also one of the most effective development tools available.

Sit down with the salesperson and watch the interaction together. Not to embarrass them—to show them what the customer saw. Most salespeople have no idea what their resting expression looks like, or that they hover, or that their eyes go to the next car on the lot mid-conversation. Seeing it once is worth a month of telling.

Set the Culture

Body language isn't just an individual issue. It's a culture issue. If your showroom has salespeople lounging visibly when customers walk by, debating in earshot whose turn it is, or dragging themselves onto the lot like it's a burden — that's a management problem.

The standard you walk past is the standard you accept. Hold the line on professional presence, not as a rule to enforce but as a culture to build. Customers feel the energy of a room the moment they walk in. Make sure they feel they're part of a team that wants to be there.

The Simplest Coaching Note

If you had one thing to tell your team every morning, it would be this: slow down. Most body language problems — the sprint, the hover, the rushed greeting, the fidgeting — come from internal urgency leaking out physically. When a salesperson slows their body down, almost everything else improves with it.

Slow down. Stand up straight. Look at people. Give them room.

That's the whole coaching note. The rest is reinforcement.

Appendix - The Rules

Every chapter in this book ends with The Rule — the single most important principle from that chapter. Here they are collected in one place for quick reference.

Introduction

"The Rule: The sale begins the moment the customer sees you. Everything your body does from that point forward is part of the presentation."

Chapter 1 — Why Body Language Matters More Than Your Words

"The Rule: When what your body says contradicts what your mouth says, the customer believes your body. Make sure they're saying the same thing."

Chapter 2 — The First Thing Customers See

"The Rule: The customer sees you before you see them. What they see in those first moments determines whether the conversation is starting uphill or downhill."

Chapter 3 — Posture: What Standing Like You Mean It Does for a Sale

"The Rule: Your posture is broadcasting your confidence level to every customer who can see you. Make sure what they're receiving is what you intend to send."

Chapter 4 — Eye Contact: The Line Between Confident and Creepy

"The Rule: Look at people when you're talking to them and when they're talking to you. Natural eye contact builds trust. Avoiding it kills credibility. Overdoing it kills comfort."

Chapter 5 — The Handshake and the First Touch

"The Rule: The handshake is the first physical statement you make. Firm, full, brief. Then step back and give them room."

Chapter 6 — Pace and Movement: How You Walk the Lot

"The Rule: Your pace tells customers whether you're chasing them or guiding them. Slow down. Walk with them. Let the lot feel like a conversation, not a foot race."

Chapter 7 — Facial Expression: What Your Face Is Doing When You Think Nobody's Looking

"The Rule: Your face is part of the presentation. Know what it's doing. A genuine expression opens doors. A checked-out expression closes them — usually before you've said a word."

Chapter 8 — Reading the Customer's Body Language

"The Rule: Stop running your own internal script long enough to actually watch the person in front of you. Customers tell you everything you need to know. Most salespeople just aren't listening with their eyes."

Chapter 9 — Open vs. Closed: What Customer Posture Tells You

"The Rule: Open posture is an invitation. Closed posture is a signal to back off, not push through. Read it correctly and respond to what's actually happening, not what you wish were happening."

Chapter 10 — The Signals That Say They're Ready

"The Rule: When the customer is ready, they'll tell you — with their body, their questions, and their language. Your job is to be watching closely enough to hear it."

Chapter 11 — Common Body Language Mistakes Salespeople Make

"The Rule: Bad body language habits are invisible to the person who has them and obvious to every customer who experiences them. Find yours. Fix them. The floor will tell you everything if you're paying attention."

Chapter 12 — Using Space: Distance, Positioning, and Presence

"The Rule: Space is part of the conversation. Give customers room to breathe, and they'll stay longer. Crowd them, and they'll find a reason to leave."

Chapter 13 — The Body Language Checklist

"The Rule: Awareness is the whole game. Know what your body is doing. Know what the customer's body is doing. Respond to reality, not assumptions. That's the checklist in one sentence."

Also Available

The Complete Car Sales Survival Guide

The No-BS Playbook for New Automotive Salespeople

Car Sales Survival Guide Series:

Book 1 — The Meet and Greet Playbook

How to Make Powerful First Impressions with Customers, Clients, and Guests

Book 2 — The First 60 Seconds in Car Sales

A Proven Meet and Greet System to Build Trust and Start More Conversations

Book 3 — How to Handle "I'm Just Looking" in Car Sales

A Simple System to Turn Brush-Offs into Productive Conversations

Book 4 — Body Language in Car Sales

How Posture, Eye Contact, and Presence Build Customer Trust

Book 5 — Greeting Customers on the Lot

How to Approach Buyers Without Pressure

Book 6 — The Ten-Second Rule in Car Sales

Why First Impressions Determine Whether Customers Stay or Leave

Book 7 — The Car Sales Conversation Starter Guide

How to Begin Natural Conversations That Lead to Sales

Book 8 — Car Sales Confidence for New Salespeople

How to Approach Customers Without Fear or Hesitation

Book 9 — Common Car Sales Greeting Mistakes

What Drives Customers Away in the First Minute

Book 10 — The First Five Minutes With a Car Buyer
How to Transition from Greeting to Conversation and Move Toward the Sale

WORK WITH BRUCE

If you're interested in one-on-one coaching, sales team training, or dealership consulting, Bruce works with individuals and organizations through Life Guidance Consulting.

For inquiries:

www.lifeguidanceconsulting.com

bruce@lifeguidanceconsulting.com

For publishing inquiries or bulk orders:

www.bedrockheritagepublishing.com

info@bedrockheritagepublishing.com

About the Author

Bruce Huddleston spent thirty-five years in the automotive industry, working every level of the business from showroom floor salesperson to finance manager, sales manager, used car manager, and general manager. His career included new-car franchise dealerships, independent used-car operations, and a decade in buy-here, pay-here — giving him a breadth of experience that few in the industry can match.

He began as a high school dropout who needed a job and ended up discovering a profession. He ended as a veteran who had trained hundreds of salespeople, managed multiple departments, and built a reputation for straight talk in an industry that doesn't always reward it.

Since retiring, Bruce has opened a life coaching practice, assists his wife with her mental health therapy practice, and operates Bedrock Heritage Publishing, a division of Life Guidance Consulting LLC, where he writes practical guides for sales professionals across multiple industries.

The Complete Car Sales Survival Guide is his flagship work. The Car Sales Survival Guide Series — a collection of focused training guides on specific sales skills — is built on the same foundation of real experience, honest insight, and zero tolerance for the kind of nonsense that gives sales a bad name.

He lives in Tyler, Texas.

A Quick Favor

If *Body Language in Car Sales* helped you — if it changed how you walk onto a lot, how you read a customer, or how you think about what your body is saying before you open your mouth — I'd be grateful if you'd take two minutes to leave a review wherever you bought it.

Reviews matter more than most people realize. They help other salespeople find books that can actually make a difference in their work. And honest feedback helps me keep writing things worth reading.

You can simply scan the QR code below.

*https://www.amazon.co
m/review/create-review/?
asin=1972179128*

https://www.amazon.com/review/create-review/?asin=1972179128
www.bedrockheritagepublishing.com
Thank you for spending time with this book. Now go to work.

— Bruce Huddleston

www.ingramcontent.com/pod-product-compliance
Lightning Source LLC
Chambersburg PA
CBHW051415050726
47595CB00010B/4077